STARS

RISING

THE 10 BEST YOUNG PLAYERS IN THE NBA

A SPORTS ILLUSTRATED FOR KIDS BOOK

Rising Stars: The 10 Best Young Players in the NBA by Glenn Nelson, Dalton Ross, and Andrea Whittaker
A SPORTS ILLUSTRATED FOR KIDS publication/December 1999

SPORTS ILLUSTRATED FOR KIDS and **KiDS** are registered trademarks of Time Inc.

Edited by Ron Berler
Front-cover and interior design by Emily Peterson Perez
Cover photographs by Andy Hayt/NBA Photos (Kobe Bryant), Nathaniel S. Butler/NBA Photos (Tim Duncan), Jesse D. Garrabrant/NBA Photos (Allen Iverson)
Additional photographs: Sports Illustrated: 6, 16, 61 (John W. McDonough); 25, 42 (Bob Rosato); 34, 52, 70 (Al Tielemans); 79 (John Biever); 88 (V.J. Lovero)

Rising Stars: The 10 Best Young Players in the NBA is published by SPORTS ILLUSTRATED FOR KIDS, a division of Time Inc. Its trademark is registered in the U.S. Patent and Trademark Office and in other countries. SPORTS ILLUSTRATED FOR KIDS, 1271 Avenue of the Americas, New York, N.Y. 10020

For information, address: SPORTS ILLUSTRATED FOR KIDS

ISBN 1-886749-81-7

Printed in the United States of America

10 9 8 7 6 5 4 3 2 1

Rising Stars: The 10 Best Young Players in the NBA is a
production of SPORTS ILLUSTRATED FOR KIDS Books:
Cathrine Wolf, Assistant Managing Editor; Emily Peterson Perez, Art Director;
Amy Lennard Goehner and Margaret Sieck, Senior Editors;
Sherie Holder, Associate Editor; Nina Gaskin, Designer; Kathleen Fieffe, Reporter;
Robert J. Rohr, Copy Editor; Erin Tricarico, Photo Researcher; Ron Beuzenburg,
Production Manager

CONTENTS

For my inspiration — Sassia, Mika, and Florangela. For my vision — Mom and Dad.
— *Glenn Nelson*

For Christina — my wife and WNBA fan extraordinaire — for everything she does for me, each and every day.
— *Dalton Ross*

For Meredith Hale and Gary Sussman.
— *Andrea Whittaker*

INTRODUCTION

When Michael Jordan retired before the 1998-99 season, many basketball fans wondered if any player would ever capture their heart again. If you have watched basketball since then, you know the answer is *yes!* There are great young players blossoming all over the NBA.

Los Angeles Laker guard Kobe Bryant reminds fans of former Laker great Magic Johnson, while high-flying Toronto Raptor guard/forward Vince Carter makes eye-popping dunks like Michael's. San Antonio forward Tim Duncan sparked the Spurs to the 1999 NBA title. And forward Kevin Garnett of the Minnesota Timberwolves has simply changed the way his position is played!

But there's more. Slick young guards Allen Iverson, Jason Williams, Stephon Marbury, and Jason Kidd make moves that spectators can hardly believe. Forwards Shareef Abdur-Rahim and Keith Van Horn are turning heads, too.

In *Rising Stars,* you'll learn about all 10 players. You'll discover the challenges they faced and overcame. You'll learn about their secret dreams and happiest days. Most of all, you will learn about the heart and dedication that it took for them to succeed — in basketball and in life.

Kobe makes
moves that
leave
opponents
shaking their
heads in
disbelief.

KOBE BRYANT

In a city of stars, he shines the brightest
★★★★★★★★★★★

Kobe Bryant has *star* written all over him. It's in the sly, cocky smile that plays on his face. It's in the gold of his Los Angeles Laker home uniform, which he wears like a royal robe.

Most of all, it's in the elegant way he flies to the basket, as if he were a 6-foot-7, 210-pound Olympic gymnast, dazzling even his opponents with his moves. He makes the game look so easy. He will flick his hand in front of a rival to steal a pass, then score on a move so smooth that he leaves fellow players shaking their heads in disbelief.

Kobe is the youngest player ever to start an NBA game and the youngest ever selected to play in the NBA All-Star Game. He did both before he was 20 years old. "It's like a dream come true," Kobe said.

He's right — it *is* a dream, of sorts. But it's a dream that came true because of years of hard work. Work that not

RISING

even his teammates always see. Kobe still pretty much lives in the gym. He is still improving. How good can he be? "I'm just getting started," he said.

Growing up in Italy
★★★★★★★★★★★★

Kobe was born August 23, 1978, in Philadelphia, Pennsylvania. His father, Joe "Jellybean" Bryant, was a smart, hard-nosed forward who played for the Philadelphia 76ers, the Houston Rockets, and the San Diego Clippers over eight NBA seasons, from 1975 to 1983. When Kobe was 3 years old, Kobe would play along with a Nerf ball and mini-basket while watching his father play on TV.

"Right away, he started dunking," Kobe's mother, Pam, recalled. "I said, 'Sweetheart, you'll break the basket. Don't dunk. Just shoot jump shots and layups.' He'd have his little cup of Gatorade and his towel, and he'd say, 'Mom, I'm sweating.' "

Joe's NBA career ended when Kobe was 5. But Joe didn't want to stop playing. He accepted an offer to join a pro team in Italy. He and Pam decided that living in Europe would be a great learning experience — not only for them, but also for Kobe and his two older sisters, Shaya and Sharia.

The family spent eight years in Italy. Kobe loved it there. He learned to speak Italian fluently, and he excelled in school. In his free time, he devoted himself to basketball. He followed his father's career, of course, but he practiced and studied the game largely on his own.

Kobe spent hours studying tapes of Los Angeles Laker games. Most of the tapes came by mail from his grandparents, in the U.S. Kobe's favorite player was Magic Johnson, who helped lead the Lakers to five NBA titles. Magic was a sky-walking acrobat who played with energy, passion, and sheer joy. Kobe tried to play like that.

"I watched Magic and [Boston Celtic star forward Larry] Bird, Michael [Jordan], and Dominique Wilkins [a top forward nicknamed The Human Highlight Film]," Kobe said. "They added to my game. That's where all the creativity came from. I would imagine myself playing against somebody and doing a move I saw them do on videotape."

High school player of the year
★★★★★★★★★★★

In 1991, when Kobe was 13, his parents decided to return to Philadelphia. Joe and Pam wanted to enroll their children in American schools, to prepare them for college in the U.S.

At first, Kobe didn't fit in. "I was the little kid with the Italian accent and the Italian game," he said. But he started adding some street moves to his game — for instance, 360-degree spins to glide past defenders. They won him acceptance and admiration from the other kids.

In 1992, Kobe entered Lower Merion High School, in Ardmore, Pennsylvania. Kobe knew by then that he wanted to be a pro basketball player. The first time Coach Gregg Downer saw him play, he knew Kobe was special.

RISING

STAT CITY
KOBE BRYANT

★**Team:** Los Angeles Lakers ★**Position:** Guard

★**Acquired:** Drafted No. 13 overall by Charlotte Hornets, in 1996, and traded to Los Angeles Lakers for Vlade Divac

★**Born:** August 23, 1978, in Philadelphia, Pennsylvania

★**Height:** 6-foot-7 ★**Weight:** 215 pounds

★**High School:** Lower Merion (Pennsylvania)

★**Career Bests:** 38 points (against Orlando, 3-21-99), 6 steals (against Sacramento, 4-7-99)

★**Honors:** Youngest player ever selected to NBA All-Star team, 1998; 1997 All-Rookie Second Team

★**Personal:** Single; enjoys reading and playing video games; favorite all-time movie is *Star Wars*.

"After five minutes, I said 'This kid is going to be a pro,'" Coach Downer said. "Never was there one moment I doubted that."

Kobe made the varsity team his freshman year. By the time he was a junior, he had made a local name for himself. In 1995-96, his senior season, he led Lower Merion to a 31–3 record and its first state championship in 53 years. Kobe scored 50 points in one game! He averaged 30.8 points, 12 rebounds, 6.5 assists, 3.8 blocks, and 4 steals per game for the season. By the end of his high school career, Kobe had replaced NBA great Wilt Chamberlain as the top high school scorer in Southeastern Pennsylvania history.

But it wasn't just Kobe's game skills that set him apart. "He's a motivator," said Rob Schwartz, one of his high school teammates. "Even though he was the best player on our team, he always worked hard. One time, he broke his nose at practice. He got up, and with one eye closed, shot with his left hand and hit a three-pointer. It was amazing."

After the season, Kobe was named by both *USA Today* and *Parade* magazine as the nation's High School Player of the Year. He was also selected to the McDonald's All-America Team. A number of top colleges recruited him, including Duke University, the University of Michigan, and the University of North Carolina.

A dream come true
★★★★★★★★★★★

But since ninth grade, Kobe's goal had been to do what only four players had ever done: jump from high school directly to the NBA. Three retired years ago — Moses Malone, Darryl Dawkins, and Bill Willoughby. Only Kevin Garnett was currently playing. All four were big men. No guard had ever before made that leap. At the time, Kobe was a 6-foot-5 guard.

But Kobe had a second goal. His two childhood heroes, Magic and Michael, had returned to the NBA. "I wanted to get in the league and play against those guys," he said.

RISING

Kobe's parents believed that Kobe was good enough — and mature enough — to play in the NBA. So on April 29, 1996, Kobe announced that he would enter the 1996 draft. Los Angeles Laker general manager Jerry West was interested. He invited Kobe to Los Angeles and put him through a series of drills. Jerry, a Hall of Fame player, knows talent. When Kobe finished, Jerry said, "He's simply the best prospect who ever worked out for us."

The Lakers struck a draft-day deal with the Charlotte Hornets. Charlotte made Kobe the number 13 pick overall and immediately traded him to Los Angeles for center Vlade Divac. Not only was Kobe in the NBA, he was playing for his favorite team!

A rookie's ups and downs
★★★★★★★★★★★

K obe was barely 18 years old when the 1996-97 season began. He spent much of the early part of the season on the bench. Laker coach Del Harris knew that Kobe was an excellent ball handler who could shoot from almost anywhere. And he could leap above taller players to dunk. But Kobe was still learning how to be more of a team player, and Coach Harris didn't want to rush him.

Slowly, Kobe started getting more court time. On January 28, 1997, against the Dallas Mavericks, he became the youngest player ever to start an NBA game. He was 18. He caught everyone's attention during the 1997 NBA All-Star Weekend, when he won the slam-dunk contest and scored 31 points in the Rookie All-Star Game. "It's going to be scary when he's 24, 25, 26," said teammate Shaquille O'Neal, after watching him. "It's going to be *real* scary."

By playoff time, Kobe was playing close to 20 minutes per game. He was so athletic that he played three different positions: point guard, shooting guard, and small forward. Coach Harris began to turn to him in clutch situations.

But in a crucial game in the second playoff round, Kobe shot four air balls in the closing minutes against the Utah Jazz. The Lakers lost, ending their season. Kobe felt that he was to blame. It was the type of experience that can rattle a player's confidence. Many around Kobe — including Magic Johnson — were curious to see how the young player would respond.

It didn't take long to find out. A few hours after the team returned to Los Angeles, Kobe walked into the gym. "That

Kobe's Hall of Fame Double

Like Magic Johnson, the Lakers' joyous, acrobatic star of the 1980's and 1990's, there is something about Kobe that sets him apart from other players and makes him hard not to like. Growing up, Kobe studied tapes of Magic's games for hours. He watched Magic's ball-handling skills, shooting touch, and personality and built them into his own game. Like Magic, too, Kobe is a tall guard who can play almost any position on the court.

RISING

was just like me," Magic said. "This is where he needs to be."

Said Kobe, "Those air balls didn't bother me. Give the ball to me right now in that situation, and I'd take a shot again." In fact, Kobe did just that. In his first trip back to Utah the following season, he blocked what would have been a game-tying shot by one of the Jazz players. Then he made a memorable dunk to win the game!

In 1998, Kobe became the youngest player ever selected to the All-Star team. He finished the 1997-98 season averaging 15.4 points per game, more than double the 7.6 points per game he averaged in his rookie season.

Learning never stops
★★★★★★★★★★★

By 1999, Kobe's third season, Michael had retired and Kobe had replaced him as the NBA's most popular star. Again, he helped lead the Lakers to the playoffs, averaging 19.9 points per game. And again, the Lakers lost, this time to the San Antonio Spurs, who went on to win the title. Kobe decided he had to work even harder.

When former Bull coach Phil Jackson was named the Lakers' new boss, in June 1999, Kobe was one of the first to call him. Teach me the game, he told Phil. Teach me what I don't know. There might not be another sports star as humble and as hungry as Kobe is.

"Basketball is kind of like life," Kobe said. "You can get knocked on your butt. But you have to get up and hold your head high and try again. That's how I'm going to be."

TIM DUNCAN

He doesn't need to yell and shout. His game says it all.

★★★★★★★★★★★

While his San Antonio Spur teammates celebrated madly on court, Tim Duncan raced for his video camera. The Spurs had just won the 1999 NBA title and Tim wanted to document the moment. "I'm keeping it on tape," he said. "It's a blessing to get where I am now."

Who could blame Tim for wanting to preserve this special moment? He had led the Spurs to the title, averaging 27.4 points and 14 rebounds per game during the five-game Final series with the New York Knicks. It was the Spurs' first title in their 32-year history. For Tim, it was the crowning moment in his journey from being a shy, clumsy kid from a small island to being the Number One player in the world.

Tim was born April 25, 1976, on the island of St. Croix, in the U.S. Virgin Islands. (The Virgin Islands are in the Caribbean Sea, near Puerto Rico.) By age 13, Tim was

15

Tim led the Spurs past everyone to their first-ever NBA title, in 1999.

16

already a great athlete. But his main sport was swimming. His whole family — which included a brother and two sisters — were swimmers. Tim had hardly played basketball.

Tim was a top freestyle swimmer. His older sister, Tricia, went on to swim for the Virgin Islands in the 1988 Olympics. "Timmy was even better than me," Tricia said. "There is no doubt in my mind that he would have gone to the 1992 Olympics and held his own against the world."

But then, on September 17, 1989, Hurricane Hugo hit St. Croix. The storm had destroyed the only Olympic-sized pool on the island. Tim's swim team was forced to hold practices in the ocean. "Tim was not happy about swimming in the ocean," his father, William, said. "He was afraid of the sharks." So he gave up the sport.

Mr. Clumsy
★★★★★★★★★★

For awhile, Tim had no special sport. That changed a year later. Tim's mother, Ione, died of breast cancer. Tim's older sister Cheryl and her husband, Ricky Lowery, moved back to St. Croix from Ohio to help care for the family. Ricky got Tim interested in basketball, partly to help him get Tim's mind off his mother's death.

There were only four indoor basketball courts on the entire island, but Tim and Ricky practiced on them constantly. At first, Tim was so awkward with the ball that Ricky nicknamed him Mr. Clumsy. Tim improved slowly. But he *grew* quickly. While he was in high school, at St.

RISING

Dunstan's Episcopal High, he grew eight inches, to 6-foot-9.

Tim's big break came in the summer of 1992, when he was 16. A group of NBA rookies had come to the Virgin Islands to help promote basketball. Tim got to play in a game with Alonzo Mourning, who went on to become the star center for the Miami Heat. Tim performed so well that another of the touring players told his college coach about him. The college was Wake Forest University, and the coach was Dave Odom. Coach Odom soon flew to St. Croix. He watched Tim play and immediately offered him a scholarship!

A promise to his mother
★★★★★★★★★★★

Tim had grown to 6-foot-10 and 200 pounds by the start of his freshman season at Wake Forest. But since he had played basketball for just a few years, he was still rough around the edges. In his first game, against the University of Alaska at Anchorage, Tim went scoreless. He didn't even attempt a shot!

But Tim was a quick and eager learner. In his sophomore season, he scored 16 points and grabbed 20 rebounds to help lead Wake Forest to an upset win over the University of North Carolina. The victory gave Wake Forest its first Atlantic Coast Conference tournament title in 32 years.

"He learned faster than anyone I've ever coached," Coach Odom said. Tim averaged 19.1 points and 12.3 rebounds per game in his junior year, and was named the

ACC Player of the Year. Had he wanted, he could have left college then for the NBA. Most experts said he would have been the number one pick and could have pocketed millions of dollars. But Tim chose to remain at Wake Forest.

One reason he stayed was that he had promised his mother he would graduate from college. The other was that he simply loved being at Wake Forest. "I was having

STAT CITY
TIMOTHY THEODORE DUNCAN

★**Team:** San Antonio Spurs   ★**Position:** Forward

★**Acquired:** Drafted No. 1 overall by San Antonio in 1997

★**Born:** April 25, 1976, in St. Croix, U.S. Virgin Islands, an island near Puerto Rico

★**Height:** 7 feet   ★**Weight:** 248 pounds

★**College:** Wake Forest University

★**Career Bests:** 39 points (against Vancouver, 4/1/99), 22 rebounds (against Chicago, 11/3/98)

★**Honors:** 1999 NBA Finals MVP; All-NBA First Team, 1998-99, 1997-98; 1998 NBA All-Star; 1997-98 NBA Rookie of the Year

★**Personal:** Single; likes to play practical jokes and video games

RISING

fun in college," Tim said. "And I was still growing up."

In his senior year, Tim simply dominated on the basketball court. He became the first player in ACC history to lead the conference in scoring, rebounding, field-goal percentage, *and* blocked shots, all in one year. His combination of size, strength, speed, and shooting skill earned him several national player-of-the-year awards.

Teaming with David Robinson
★★★★★★★★★★

The San Antonio Spurs were thrilled that Tim had stayed in school. The Spurs had been one of the league's best teams during the 1990's, but they had tumbled to a 20–62 record in 1996-97 because of injuries. David Robinson, their All-Star center, missed almost the entire season. The Spurs ended up with the number one pick in the 1997 NBA draft, and they chose Tim. There was more good news: By the start of the 1997-98 season, all their players, including David, were healthy.

The Spurs knew that Tim had talent, but even *they* were surprised by his skill. Shortly after the draft, David invited Tim to his Colorado home to practice. He was amazed by Tim's technique. "He's everything he was advertised to be," David said. "But what I didn't expect was his tremendous passing. Wow!"

On offense and on defense, Tim could do it all! He had grown to be 7 feet and weighed 248 pounds. That made him strong enough to play close to the basket. But he also had a nice, soft shooting touch from outside. Michael Jordan, for one, was impressed. In Tim's third NBA game, he went head-to-head with Michael and the NBA champion Chicago Bulls. Tim scored 19 points and grabbed 22 rebounds. Afterward, Michael said, "I can see why he went number one [in the draft]. He stayed those four years in college and the payoff for doing that is starting to show."

Tim had one of the best rookie seasons in NBA history. He averaged 21.1 points, 11.9 rebounds, and 2.5 blocked shots per game. He was the third player ever to be named Rookie of the Month for all six months of the season, and was named the NBA Rookie of the Year.

More important, Tim teamed with David to form a "Twin Towers" combination that made the Spurs a power-house. In Tim's first year, San Antonio improved its record by 36 wins. That was the biggest jump in NBA history! In the playoffs, the team advanced all the way to the Western Conference semi-finals, before losing to the Utah Jazz.

The road to the NBA Finals
★★★★★★★★★★★★

Still, people questioned Tim's ability to lead the Spurs to the next level, the NBA Finals. After 14 games in the 1999 season, the team was a disappointing 6–8. Critics wondered about Tim's passion to win. Even one of Tim's teammates, Mario Elie, questioned his desire. Tim waited until after the season to respond.

RISING

Tim's Hall of Fame Double

Kareem Abdul-Jabbar was the greatest center of the 1970's and 1980's. He led the Milwaukee Bucks to one championship and the Los Angeles Lakers to five more. Like Kareem, Tim does his job quietly, with a minimum of fuss. He is strong and quick, and often uses Kareem's favorite weapons: the jump hook shot, the skyhook, and the power move inside. Both stayed in school and earned their college degrees.

Tim had majored in psychology *[sigh-COLL-o-gee]* in college. He said he had taken what he had learned about how people's minds work and used it in his game. "If you show disappointment or frustration [on the court, and] your opponent picks up on this, you are at a disadvantage," he wrote in *Sport* magazine. "I make sure opponents don't know what's going on in my head."

In a league filled with emotional show-offs, Tim is a throwback. "It's uncommon for someone his age to be so competitive, yet poised," Spur coach Gregg Popovich said.

Teammate Will Perdue agreed. About the only time Tim shows emotion, Will said, is when he's "kicking somebody's behind in Sony PlayStation."

Led by Tim, the Spurs recovered from their 6–8 start. They went 31–5 the rest of the season. Tim was spectacular. He beat teams under the basket. He beat them from outside, with his skyhook and bank shots. He beat them on defense with quick feet and an intimidating presence. He averaged 21.7 points, 11.4 rebounds, and 2.5 blocks per game, and finished third in voting for the league's Most Valuable Player. But Tim's regular-season play was nothing compared to what he would do in the post-season.

In the opening round of the playoffs, Tim and the Spurs made quick work of the Minnesota Timberwolves. Then they swept the Los Angeles Lakers in four games. Tim averaged 29 points and 10.8 rebounds per game. Next, the Spurs swept the Portland Trailblazers.

"The best player in the NBA"
★★★★★★★★★★★

Tim had led the team to its first-ever NBA Finals, against the New York Knicks. The Spurs won that series, four games to one. Tim was named the MVP of the Finals. He averaged 23.2 points, 11.5 rebounds, and 2.6 blocks per game over the course of the playoffs.

"He's obviously the best player in the NBA," Knick coach Jeff Van Gundy said afterward. "You can just watch a guy play and know if he's truly into winning or not. That guy's truly into winning."

All the swimming practices, the discipline and determination, the basketball lessons from Ricky, the four years of college ball: They had all finally paid off. Tim was now a champion.

Mr. Clumsy was clumsy no more.

STEPHON MARBURY

The hardest-working player in the NBA

★★★★★★★★★★★

Stephon Marbury lives in a home in the wealthy town of Alpine, New Jersey. Every so often, though, he returns to his family's old apartment in the Coney Island section of Brooklyn, New York.

Up four flights of dirty stairs and down a dark, cinder-block hallway is the simple home that the New Jersey Nets' star point guard lived in when he was growing up. Getting his family out of that 15-story Surfside Garden housing project is what drove Stephon to make it to the NBA.

A few years ago, Stephon moved his parents far from Coney Island, to a quiet Maryland suburb. But the Marburys still keep the apartment in Surfside Garden. And Stephon keeps going back to Brooklyn to visit it. Returning to the apartment reminds Stephon of where he has come from. It reminds him how hard he worked to get out of

Stephon had to fight
for everything he has.
Even against bigger
players, he refuses
to lose.

25

RISING

Surfside Garden and how hard he must work to continue to be one of the most electrifying players in the NBA.

"I'm always going to come back," said Stephon. "It helps keep me real, no doubt."

Talent isn't enough
★★★★★★★★★★★

tephon was born February 20, 1977. He is one of seven children. His father, Donald, Senior, was a construction worker who sometimes couldn't find work. His mother, Mabel, worked in a day-care center. There was never much money. Stephon had three older brothers. The family's dream was that one of the brothers would make it to the NBA and rescue them all from poverty.

The oldest Marbury brother, Eric, was 17 when Stephon was born. He came close to making the NBA. He was a hard-nosed guard who played at the University of Georgia, with future NBA star Dominique Wilkins. But Eric was cut by the San Diego Clippers during training camp, in 1982. He couldn't catch on with any other teams. So he moved back to Brooklyn and became an ironworker. And he started coaching his younger brothers, hoping one of *them* would make it.

"Maybe I wasn't good enough," Eric said. "But ever since my brothers were small, I made sure they all knew the commitment it would take for them to make it."

Eric worked first with Donald, Junior, called Donnie, and then with Norman, known as "Jou-Jou." They didn't make the NBA, either. Their chances were hurt when poor grades cost them big-time college scholarships. Donnie, a shooting guard, eventually played two years at Texas A&M University. Jou-Jou, a point guard, played one season at St. Francis College, in Brooklyn.

Three Marbury brothers had come out of Brooklyn's Abraham Lincoln High School billed as superstars. All had failed to make it to the NBA. The family began to get a reputation of being underachievers. Eric didn't want Stephon to be another Marbury underachiever. Luckily, Stephon shared his brother's fierce determination to succeed.

Brother knows best
★★★★★★★★★★★

Anybody could see that Stephon had talent. When he was 3 years old, his father took him to the University of Georgia to watch Eric play. During a team practice, he scampered out to center court, picked up a ball, dribbled it to the basket, and laid it in. At age 9, he was performing shooting exhibitions during halftime at Lincoln High's games. When he turned 11, *Hoop Scoop*, a national basketball magazine, named him the best sixth-grade player in the country!

Eric developed a strict training program for Stephon. Each day after school, Stephon ran sprints along Coney Island's beach, then raced three times up and down the 15 floors of his apartment building.

Part of his training was doing well in school. Stephon was determined not to be derailed by poor grades, as

RISING

Donnie and Jou-Jou had been. He never questioned Eric's plan. "I knew everything he told me would make me better," Stephon said. Like all his brothers, Stephon wore Eric's uniform number, 3.

Mr. New York Basketball
★★★★★★★★★★★

By the time Stephon entered Lincoln High, in 1991, he was one of the most talked about prospects in New York City basketball. The skills that would eventually carry him to the NBA were already developing — the startling quickness, the excellent ball-handling skills, the deadly accurate jump-shooting, the terrific passing ability.

Stephon lived up to his billing. For three straight seasons, he led the school to the city's championship game. In 1994-95, his senior year, he averaged 28 points, 9.5 assists, and 3.5 steals per game. In the title game, Stephon scored 26 points — including two game-clinching free throws with 11 seconds remaining — to lead Lincoln to a 61–56 victory.

There was more. Two weeks later, Stephon scored 28 points to lead Lincoln to its first state high school championship. He was named a *Parade* magazine High School All-America, and Mr. New York Basketball! That fall, in 1995, Stephon enrolled at Georgia Tech University. He started his freshman season with a bang. In his first game, he scored 16 points to lead Georgia Tech to a win over Manhattan College, despite battling tonsillitis and a 102-degree fever. "Stephon doesn't walk on water," said Fran

Frashilla, Manhattan's coach at the time, "but he doesn't get very wet, either."

Against Georgetown University and its standout guard Allen Iverson a few days later, Stephon turned heads with his quickness and his no-look passes. He had 13 points, 8 assists, and 7 steals. Stephon led the Yellow Jackets to the Atlantic Coast Conference title, averaging a team-high 18.9 points per game. He became just the fifth freshman in ACC history to be selected to the All-Conference team! Stephon was named a third-team All-America.

Stephon and Kevin
★★★★★★★★★★★

Soon after the season ended, Stephon announced that he would leave Georgia Tech and enter the 1996 NBA draft. Milwaukee selected Stephon number four overall and traded him the same day to the Minnesota Timberwolves. Stephon was ecstatic. A Marbury had finally made it! His family wept with joy.

Stephon couldn't believe his good fortune. He already had a friend on the Wolves: Kevin Garnett. The two had played together during high school on the U.S. Junior National Select Team. For several years, they had phoned each other regularly to talk about their NBA dreams. Now they would be teammates. Together with top-scoring forward Tom Gugliotta, they would be something!

Stephon was only 19 years old, but he proved himself almost immediately. In December, he put on a dominating performance against All-Star guard John Stockton and the Utah Jazz, with 33 points and 8 assists. For the season, he averaged 15.8 points and 7.9 assists per game and finished second to Allen Iverson in voting for 1997 Rookie of the Year. More important, he helped lead the Wolves to the playoffs for the first time in franchise history.

The following season, 1997-98, Stephon performed even better. He averaged 17.7 points and 8.6 assists per game. That year, the NBA All-Star Game was played in his hometown, New York City. Stephon thought he would be selected for the game. But he wasn't. That failure made him think about the short distance that separated Madison Square Garden from his family's poor Brooklyn apartment. Stephon decided to work at his game even harder.

Going home
★★★★★★★★★★★

After the All-Star Game, Stephon went on a tear. He averaged 26.2 points over the next six games! He helped carry the Wolves back to the playoffs.

In Game 2 of the first round, against the Seattle SuperSonics, Stephon put on the best performance of his career. He scored 25 points, had 7 assists, and made 2 steals to lead the Wolves to a 98–93 win, their first playoff victory! Minnesota won another game before being eliminated.

Stephon and the Wolves seemed one solid player away from becoming one of the NBA's elite teams. But it wasn't to be. Instead, Tom Gugliotta left after the season to play for the Phoenix Suns. With Tom gone, Minnesota decided to rebuild completely. On March 11, 1999, as part of a three-team trade, the Wolves sent Stephon to New Jersey.

Stephon had always dreamed of playing near home. Now he was back, close to his Brooklyn roots. His happiness showed in his game. On April 25, 1999, against the Indiana Pacers, he had a career-high 20 assists. Ten days later, playing the Milwaukee Bucks, he scored a career-high 41 points. He finished the 1998-99 season averaging 21.3 points per game — eighth best in the NBA. He ranked third in assists, with 8.9 per game.

After the season, Stephon signed a long-term contract with the Nets. Stephon's dream is to win the NBA title with a New York City-area team.

Stephon is happy. But he's still not comfortable. He still thinks of his family and all their years of struggle. So even

Stephon's Hall of Fame Double

Stephon is one of the NBA's top passers *and* scorers. Only one other point guard in NBA history had that combination of talents: Hall of Famer Nate "Tiny" Archibald. Tiny played for seven teams in the 1970's and early 1980's. Like Stephon, he was blindingly quick, and was a master of the no-look pass. Tiny was the only guard ever to lead the league in both scoring and assists in the same season. If anyone can match that feat, it's Stephon.

now, he keeps returning to the apartment in Brooklyn. It is a reminder of what his life would have been like without hard work and dedication. All he has to do is walk past the courts he played on as a kid to be reminded of all the players out there who are hungrier than he.

"I work harder now at my game than I did two years ago, because I understand that now people are going to be gunning for me," he said. "Every minute I'm not working, someone's lifting weights, someone's running, someone's shooting jump shots. That's why I can't stop."

STAT CITY
STEPHON XAVIOR MARBURY

★**Team:** New Jersey Nets ★**Position:** Guard

Acquired: Traded to New Jersey from Minnesota as part of a three-team trade, March 11, 1999

Born: February 20, 1977, in Brooklyn, New York

★**Height:** 6-foot-2 ★**Weight:** 180 pounds

College: Georgia Tech University

Career Bests: 41 points (against Milwaukee, 5-5-99), 20 assists (against Indiana, 4-25-99)

Honors: 1996-97 NBA All-Rookie First Team

Personal: Single; favorite video game is "In the Zone"; favorite performer is Notorious B.I.G.

ALLEN IVERSON

Looking for excitement? Here's "The Answer."

★★★★★★★★★★★

He calls himself "The Answer," but Allen Iverson has spent most of his career raising questions. He has raised questions in other people's minds about his attitude, his judgment, and his values. In his first two NBA seasons, the Philadelphia 76er guard was arrested once, suspended by the league once, and disciplined by his team a number of times. Michael Jordan and other great players called him a selfish hotshot who would not listen to coaches.

Many considered it a shame that Allen's attitude and behavior were getting in the way of so much talent. Because, clearly, he is one of the most exciting athletes ever to play the game. He is the most acrobatic scorer since Michael. Though he is just six feet tall, he is a ferocious dunker. His passing and ball handling are dazzling. "He's so quick, he leaves his teammates behind," said basketball Hall of Famer Dave Bing. "I don't even know that *he* knows how fast he is."

Allen's blinding quickness allows him to rise above the rest of the league.

But Allen played for himself, and his team seldom won.

Then, in 1999, he changed his act. Allen stopped getting into trouble. He showed up on time for practice — and made sure his teammates did, too. He listened more carefully to his coach. Instead of always looking to shoot the ball, he began to pass to his teammates and involve them in the game. For the first time, Allen led the Philadelphia 76ers to the playoffs. *Surprise!*

Allen had matured. At last, he seemed to be squarely on his way to a Hall of Fame career.

A football fan
★★★★★★★★★★★

Allen's path to the NBA wasn't easy. He grew up extremely poor in Hampton, Virginia. He was born June 7, 1975, the year his mother, Ann, was 15 years old. His father deserted the family soon afterward. His stepfather was in and out of jail. Allen remembers nights when he, his mother, and his sisters, Brandy and Iiesha, had no running water or electricity in their home.

For Allen, sports were an escape from his family's struggles. He threw himself into every game he played. A good player, he was determined to become a professional athlete so that he could rescue his family from poverty.

Growing up, football was Allen's favorite sport. "Still is," he said. "I didn't even want to play basketball at first. I thought it was soft. My mother's the one who made me go to tryouts. I'll thank her forever."

RISING

At Bethel High School, in Hampton, Allen starred at both. He led the school to the state football title, playing quarterback and safety. That winter, he led Bethel to the state basketball title, too! Colleges recruited Allen for both sports.

Trouble and triumph
★★★★★★★★★★★

Then Allen ran into his first trouble with the law. On the night of February 14, 1993, Allen walked into a bowling alley in Hampton, just as a wild fight broke out. Dozens of people were involved. Allen said he left the bowling alley as soon as the fight began, but two witnesses said he was one of the brawlers. He was found guilty at a trial and sentenced to five years in jail.

But Allen got a second chance! Virginia Governor L. Douglas Wilder re-examined the case. Governor Wilder found no evidence against Allen. After serving four months in jail, Allen was released, and the guilty verdict was dropped.

Questions about his reputation remained. Few colleges wanted to take a chance on Allen. But after a long talk with him, Georgetown University basketball coach John Thompson decided to offer him a scholarship. Allen responded by leading the 1994-95 Hoyas with 20.4 points and 4.5 assists per game. He was named the Big East Conference's Rookie of the Year and Defensive Player of the Year!

That's when Allen picked up the nickname The Answer. Fans started calling him that because he seemed to have a solution for any problem on the court.

A special bond formed between coach and player. Coach Thompson had been a father figure to other Georgetown stars, such as Patrick Ewing, Dikembe Mutombo, and Alonzo Mourning. Now he took Allen under his wing. "He taught me a lot of things: how to deal with people, how to deal with different situations," Allen said. "It made me feel good that he was comfortable with me. That meant a lot to me."

Allen played even better during his sophomore season. He averaged 25 points, 4.7 assists, and 3.35 steals per game,

STAT CITY
ALLEN EZAIL IVERSON

★**Team:** Philadelphia 76ers   ★**Position:** Guard

★**Acquired:** Drafted No.1 overall by Philadelphia in 1996

★**Born:** June 7, 1975, in Hampton, Virginia

★**Height:** 6 feet   ★**Weight:** 165 pounds

★**College:** Georgetown University

★**Career Bests:** 50 points (against Cleveland, 4-12-97), 15 assists (twice), 6 steals (four times)

★**Honors:** 1998-99 All-NBA First Team, 1996-97 NBA Rookie of the Year, 1995-96 First Team All-America

★**Personal:** Single; has a daughter, Tiaura, and a son, Allen II; favorite book is *The Color Purple*

RISING

and led Georgetown to the 1996 NCAA tournament. After the season, he was named a First Team All-America. He was the best point guard in college basketball!

Allen could have remained at Georgetown. But fewer than 150 miles away, his family was still living in poverty. He decided to enter the 1996 NBA draft.

Advice from Michael
★★★★★★★★★★★

The Philadelphia 76ers had the first pick in the 1996 draft. At 6 feet and 165 pounds, Allen became the smallest number one selection in the history of the draft.

His effect on the team was immediate. In Allen's first NBA game, he scored 30 points against the Milwaukee Bucks. Defenses just couldn't keep up with him. After trying — and failing — to guard Allen, Chicago Bull guard Ron Harper said, "I thought I could play defense. Now I don't know."

Unfortunately, Allen's cockiness and bad attitude were just as evident as his talent. After his hot start, he began showing up late for practice. He rarely passed the ball to his teammates. All Allen cared about, it seemed, was scoring. This rubbed a lot of players the wrong way.

During the 1997 All-Star Weekend, Michael Jordan, Patrick Ewing, and Charles Barkley urged Allen to change his attitude. But Allen wouldn't listen. Late in the season, he set an NBA record by scoring 40 or more points in five straight games. He did it shooting almost every time he got the ball, seldom passing. The 76ers lost all five games. Though Allen averaged 23.5 points per game for the season and was named Rookie of the Year, Charles Barkley was unimpressed. He called Allen "me, myself, and Iverson."

That summer, Allen got into some real trouble. Police stopped his Mercedes for speeding. Allen wasn't driving, but he was in the car. The police searched the vehicle and found marijuana and a handgun. Allen was charged with drug and firearm possession. The charges were later dropped, after Allen agreed to perform community service and undergo monthly drug tests for two years.

Allen's new teacher
★★★★★★★★★★★

Allen had been lucky to find John Thompson. Now, he got lucky again. In 1997, Larry Brown was hired as the new 76er coach. Coach Brown had been a star point guard in the old American Basketball Association. As a coach, his strength is teaching team-oriented basketball. He made Allen his special project.

Coach Brown tried to teach Allen what Chicago Bull coach Phil Jackson had taught a young Michael Jordan: that great players make their *teammates* better. But Allen grew frustrated when he made a good pass and his teammate missed the shot. He would sulk. He would report late to practice. The team disciplined him a number of times.

Slowly, though, Allen came around. And once he started passing the ball more, the number of his turnovers (times he lost the ball to the other team) went way down. For the 1997-98 season, Allen averaged 22 points, 6.2 assists, and 2.2 steals per game. His game was becoming more complete.

But the 76ers won only 31 games. So over the summer, Allen decided to be even less selfish with the ball. When the 76ers gathered to begin practice for the 1998-99 season, they saw a new Allen. Coach Brown's lessons had taken hold.

A true team player
★★★★★★★★★★★

For the first time, Allen began acting as a team leader. "I think it's my responsibility to make sure guys get in here for practice, and I will," Allen said. "I want to be here when this whole thing turns around, so that I can say I've been here and suffered and now it's my turn to shine."

Shine, he did. Coach Brown moved Allen from point guard to shooting guard. The switch freed Allen to do what he does best — find ways to score. He discovered that he could open up opportunities for himself and his teammates by passing and moving without the ball. During the first month of the season, Allen led the 76ers to an 8–5 record. It was the team's first winning month in five seasons!

Allen's new team-oriented approach helped carry the team to its first playoff appearance since 1991. He also led the NBA in scoring by averaging 26.8 points per game. He was the first 76er to win the scoring title in 30 years!

But the party wasn't over. Philadelphia faced the heavily favored Orlando Magic in the first round of the playoffs. In

Game 3, with the series tied at a game apiece, Allen scored 33 points and made an NBA playoff-record 10 steals. The 76ers won, 97–85. "I sent a message to my teammates that it's not just about scoring points," Allen said afterward. "That's something the coach has been working with me on."

Allen's Hall of Fame Double

Allen is an undersized guard with phenomenal speed, super passing ability, and the guts of an NFL running back when driving to the basket. What Hall of Famer does that sound like? Isiah Thomas, who helped the Detroit Pistons win two titles, in 1989 and 1990. In addition, Isiah and Allen both started at point guard and sometimes shifted to shooting guard. Both were great scorers. Isiah was the first player from Indiana University to leave college early for the NBA. Allen was the first Georgetown player to leave early.

Allen then scored 37 points to lead the team to a 101–91 victory that clinched the series! Coach Brown was proud. "Allen's doing what great players do," he said. "He's making other people better, and he is taking responsibility."

In the next round, Philadelphia lost to the Indiana Pacers. By the end of the playoffs, though, there were no longer any doubts. Critics who had questioned Allen's character had their "Answer."

Allen had finally made it.

Vince reminds people of his idol, Michael Jordan. It's easy to see why.

VINCE CARTER

Call him Air Canada. He's the NBA's new king of the dunk.

★★★★★★★★★★★

It was one of those all-star charity games of summer, where NBA players strut their stuff for a few minutes and then shuffle back to the bench. The host, Seattle SuperSonic star Gary Payton, played briefly. So did Magic Johnson, Penny Hardaway, and most of the rest.

But Vince Carter, the 1999 NBA Rookie of the Year, refused to leave the court. Late in the fourth quarter, the slender, 6-foot-7 guard/small forward sprinted upcourt and drilled home a 360-degree dunk. He followed that with a ringing, between-the-legs tomahawk jam. Then he delivered a scissors-kick slam. The 10,000 fans at Seattle's Key Arena leaped to their feet. The players on court responded, too. Even the opposing team wanted to see him slam.

In a league of dunking royalty, Vince is the new king. In Toronto, they call him Air Canada. "I have never seen anyone who can elevate above the rim [of the basket] like he can," said legendary NBA coach Chuck Daly. That's quite a statement from the man who coached Michael Jordan and the Dream Team in the 1992 Olympics!

Vince averaged 18.3 points per game in 1999, the best among NBA rookies. He knows he has been blessed with special skills. "From day one in the NBA," Vince said, "I felt that I was very capable and was here for a reason."

Florida's Mr. Basketball
★★★★★★★★★★★

Vince was born January 26, 1977. His mother, Michelle Carter-Robinson, and stepfather, Harry Robinson, were school teachers. Together with Vince and his younger brother, Christopher, they lived in a comfortable house in Daytona Beach, Florida. The weather there was warm enough to play outdoors year round, so Vince did! He remembers playing with a basketball at age 2.

Sports were always a big part of his life. But they weren't his whole life. Back then, Vince wasn't sure he had a future in the NBA. At 14, he was cut from his Amateur Athletic Union basketball team. The coach told him he was too slow. So, Vince worked hard to develop other, non-sports skills in which he could excel. At Daytona Beach's Mainland High School, he wrote poetry and helped compose the school's homecoming song. He was also a drum major and saxophone player in the school marching band. Vince was so good at playing the sax that he was offered a music scholarship at Bethune-Cookman College, in Daytona Beach.

Then, the summer between 10th and 11th grades, Vince grew six inches. His world changed. Almost overnight, he became one of the best high school athletes in the entire state! He was a top volleyball player and a star quarterback on the football team. During his senior year, he was named Florida's Mr. Basketball.

Vince was amazing at basketball. In one game, he scored 47 points. In another, he blocked 17 shots. Once, he injured the wrist of his right hand, his shooting hand. What did he do? He scored 32 points left-handed! Vince led his team to its first state championship in 56 years and was named a high school All-America. He leaped so high that fans started calling him U.F.O., short for Unidentified Flying Object!

Trying to be like Mike
★★★★★★★★★★★

Like a million other basketball wannabes, Vince dreamed of being like Michael Jordan. In high school, he asked to wear Michael's number 23, but a teammate already had it. Vince was heartbroken. "I told him, 'You pick another number and make it famous,'" his mother said. That's when Vince chose number 15, which he wears today.

More than 70 colleges approached Vince to play basketball for them. Following in Michael's footsteps, he chose the University of North Carolina. In many ways, Vince seemed like his hero (*see box, page 49*). His splashy style of play, shaved head, and the way he carried himself off the court reminded people of the former Chicago Bull star.

RISING

STAT CITY
VINCENT LAMAR CARTER

★**Nickname:** Air Canada

★**Team:** Toronto Raptors ★**Position:** Guard/Forward

★**Acquired:** Drafted No. 5 overall by Golden State in 1998, then traded to Toronto for Antawn Jamison

★**Born:** January 26, 1977, in Daytona Beach, Florida

★**Height:** 6-foot-7 ★**Weight:** 215 pounds

★**College:** University of North Carolina

★**Career Bests:** 32 points (against Houston, 3-25-99), 15 rebounds (against New Jersey, 3-16-99)

★**Honors:** 1999 NBA Rookie of the Year, 1997-98 Second Team All-America

★**Personal:** Single; plays alto, tenor, and baritone saxophones and trumpet

Like Michael, Vince is soft-spoken, polite, and considerate. As a child, he would give away clothes he had outgrown to needy friends. "It was Vince's way of giving," his mother said.

Unlike his idol, though, Vince was *not* an instant college star. Part of the problem was that Vince had never bothered to learn the fundamentals of the game — how to pass, how to play defense, how to move without the ball. He had depended on his high-flying skills. Vince soon learned that at the college level, those weren't enough. During his freshman year, he averaged just 7.5 points per game.

"He didn't understand that there's more to the college game than scoring and out-jumping everyone else," said Dean Smith, North Carolina's coach at the time.

Vince worked for hours, daily, on his game. Sure enough, in his sophomore year, he averaged 13 points per game and was named to the NCAA East Regional All-Tournament team.

Great player, better person
★★★★★★★★★★★

As a junior, Vince emerged as one of the top college players in the country. He led the Atlantic Coast Conference in scoring, with an average of 15.6 points per game. In the semi-final game of the NCAA tournament, he scored 21 points against the University of Utah. Still, the Tar Heels lost, 65–59. Afterward, Wake Forest University coach Dave Odom called Vince "the closest thing there is to a human highlight film in college basketball."

Vince decided that he had learned all he could at the college level. He left school to enter the 1998 NBA draft.

On June 24, 1998, the Golden State Warriors made Vince the number five pick overall. Then they traded him to the Toronto Raptors for Antawn Jamison, one of Vince's North Carolina teammates, plus cash.

Toronto coach Butch Carter knew Vince was a good player. But he didn't realize what a good person Vince is. Vince arrived in Toronto not with a gang of friends, but with a group that included his minister. He wears no tattoos or earrings. He still turns to his parents for advice. "You know right away he's not cut from the same mold as most professional athletes," said his minister, the Reverend August Sorvillo.

Welcome to the NBA!
★★★★★★★★★★★

Vince's pro debut, on February 4, 1999, was sensational. In his first game, against the Boston Celtics, he scored 16 points and grabbed three rebounds to lead Toronto to a 103–92 win!

But Vince's real test came on March 25, 1999, when the Raptors played the Rockets in Houston. There, Vince would go against Scottie Pippen, a seven-time All-Star and one of the best players in the NBA. "My assistants were saying that Pippen was going to kick Vince's butt," Coach Carter said. "So I started calling Vince's room, saying Scottie was going to send a limo to pick him up and make sure he got to the game [so that he could beat Vince]." In other words, Coach Carter was challenging Vince.

Vince responded in a big way. With Scottie guarding him, Vince scored 32 points. By the end of the game, Scottie was asking his teammates to help guard Vince.

Less than a week later, Vince beat the Indiana Pacers almost single-handedly. He had 31 points, 11 rebounds, and 6 assists — and scored the game-winning basket with 18 seconds left! The Raptors won, 88–87. "I think I had a lot of confidence from then on," Vince said afterward.

That's when the comparisons with Michael really began. Vince is about the same size as Michael, and he has Michael's huge, soft hands and tremendous upper-body strength. His powerful, slender legs give him Michael-like liftoff. People who have seen them both play say that Michael had better hang time, but that Vince jumps higher.

By the end of the 1999 season, Vince was the league's newest sensation. Fans debated Vince's greatest slams. There was his ferocious dunk over Miami's Alonzo Mourning, the 1999 NBA Defensive Player of the Year. And the body-bump-and-dunk over the game's best shot-blocker, Atlanta's Dikembe Mutombo. And the breakaway 360-degree throw-down against the Cleveland Cavaliers in the Raptors' final game. No one could decide which was best.

Vince's gravity-defying acts were so numerous, the Raptors created a special video-highlights library on their website,

Vince's Hall of Fame Double

Vince and Michael Jordan both attended the University of North Carolina, and were named NBA Rookie of the Year. Both could fly above the rim like nobody else in the game! But Vince and Michael weren't perfect. Each worked hard to become a top defensive player. Each entered the league lacking a great jump shot. Michael developed one of the best. Vince plans to do the same.

RISING

www.raptors.com. It's called the Vince Carter Jam Cam.

In a 1999 CNN-TV poll, fans named Vince the NBA's most exciting player. It's easy to see why. Vince was the only rookie to lead his team in scoring. (He averaged 18.3 points per game.) He led all guards and small forwards in blocked shots, with 1.54 per game. He was the first Raptor ever to be named NBA Player of the Week, and he won the league's Rookie of the Year award! Most important, he led the team to its best record ever and to the edge of its first playoff berth. The Raptors fell short by just four games.

Vince's summer school
★★★★★★★★★★★

During the 1999 off-season, Vince kept more than busy. He had promised his mother that he would return to the University of North Carolina to earn his degree. So, he went back to campus for summer classes. He expects to receive his degree in African-American Studies, with a minor in communications, in 2000.

Vince also attended another summer-school program all his own. He wanted to improve the one weakness in his game. Like Michael early in his career, Vince lacked a great jump shot. So, he held his own private class. Each day, he took at least *1,000* jump shots. "Some days, I might shoot 1,500," he said.

"Once he can make that 18-footer, he may be impossible to stop," Pacer coach and Hall of Famer Larry Bird said. That's bad news for Vince's opponents.

KEITH VAN HORN

He looks like a Boy Scout, but he's one tough dude

★★★★★★★★★★★

Keith Van Horn's New Jersey Nets were desperate for a win. They had already lost 10 of their first 12 games of the 1998-99 season. Now, the Nets were in danger of losing again.

The Nets were playing the Boston Celtics, in Boston. With 7.2 seconds left in the game and the score tied at 97, New Jersey guard Eric Murdoch launched a jump shot. He missed! If the Celtics were to grab the rebound, they would get the ball and a chance to set up the winning shot. The Nets would lose *again*.

But Keith didn't let that happen. The big forward grabbed the ball and dribbled to the baseline. Then, looking as if he had all the time in the world, Keith calmly put up a short jump shot. The ball bounced twice above the rim and fell through the net. The Boston crowd fell silent. The Nets went berserk. They had won, 99–97!

51

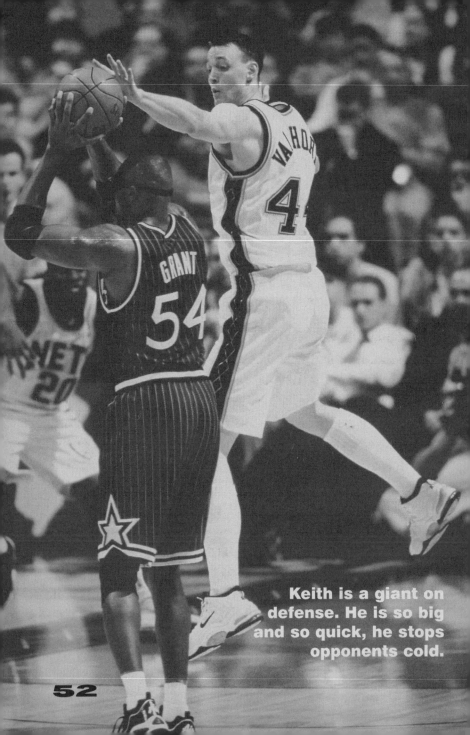

Keith is a giant on defense. He is so big and so quick, he stops opponents cold.

Keith never once doubted that the ball would go in. That coolness under fire is what made Keith the leader of the New Jersey team in his NBA rookie season. Nothing seems to fluster him.

"He wants the game-winning shot," said John Calipari, who coached the Nets during Keith's first two seasons. "There are not many veteran players in this league who want to take that responsibility."

NBA dreams
★★★★★★★★★★★

Taking responsibility has been the theme of Keith's life. His parents raised him that way. "They are my role models," he said.

Keith was born October 23, 1975, in Fullerton, California, a Los Angeles suburb. He grew up in nearby Diamond Bar. Keith's father, Ken, owned a fire sprinkler company. His mother, May, stayed at home and cared for Keith and his older brother and sister, Jeff and Kim.

"My father was always a calm and collected person," Keith said. "He never really let anything bother or upset him. He was never a yeller or anything like that. So I guess I kind of got him in my personality."

Keith's passion for basketball began early. By age 8, his dream was to play in the NBA. On weekends and during the summer, he shot hoops from sunrise to sunset. Then he would go home and watch Los Angeles Laker games on television. His bedroom walls were covered with posters of

NBA stars Magic Johnson, Michael Jordan, and Larry Bird.

Keith never tried to pattern his game after those players, though. He was smart enough to know that he lacked Larry's court vision, Magic's ball-handling skill, and Michael's jumping ability. Instead, he worked with the tools he had — quickness, strength, smarts, and speed.

"Every player establishes his own individuality in a game," Keith said. "To me, basketball is the most creative of all sports. You never see the same play twice. Just like a musician who has the freedom to make whatever music he wants, a basketball player has the freedom to create moves."

Outsmarting his opponents
★★★★★★★★★★★

At age 13, Keith stood 5-foot-10. He started playing in summer leagues in Los Angeles. He sought out the best playground games in the city. Though he looked more like a Boy Scout than an intimidating player, Keith was no pushover. He beat big players with up-and-under moves around the basket and tossed down jump shots over leaping defenders. He outsmarted opponents with head fakes that left them grabbing air, and broke to the basket with a first step that was so quick they barely saw it.

By Keith's sophomore year at Diamond Bar High School, he had grown to be 6-foot-9. In his senior year, he dominated his league. Keith averaged 29.2 points, 10.1 rebounds, and 3.7 blocks per game and was named to the

All-Western United States high school basketball team.

Keith enrolled at the University of Utah, largely because of Coach Rick Majerus. "Coach Majerus is a disciplinarian," Keith said. "But at the same time, he really cares for his players. He doesn't have children, so in some sense, we're kind of his kids and he looks after us."

Coach Majerus taught Keith NBA-style basketball. That meant learning set offensive plays and man-to-man defense. Keith flourished. As a freshman, he led the team

STAT CITY
KEITH ADAM VAN HORN

★**Team:** New Jersey Nets   ★**Position:** Forward

★**Acquired:** Drafted No. 2 overall by Philadelphia in 1997, acquired by New Jersey in an eight-player trade

★**Born:** October 23, 1975, in Fullerton, California

★**Height:** 6-foot-10   ★**Weight:** 250 pounds

★**College:** University of Utah

★**Career Bests:** 35 points (against Detroit, 2-16-99), 16 rebounds (against New York, 3-7-99)

★**Honors:** 1997-98 NBA All-Rookie First Team, 1997 First Team All-America

★**Personal:** Married to Amy Sida; has a daughter, Sabrina, and a son, Nicholas; likes to play Ping-Pong

RISING

with 18.3 points per game. He also ranked in the Top 10 among players in the Western Athletic Conference (WAC) in scoring, rebounds, 3-point goals, and blocked shots.

Setting priorities
★★★★★★★★★★★

But it wasn't an easy year for Keith. Midway through the season, his father died of heart failure. Keith was devastated. "It's hard to get over something like that at a young age," he said. "I don't know when I will get over it, but I'm sure someday I will."

During his sophomore year, Keith had another life-changing experience. His girlfriend, Amy Sida, gave birth to their daughter, Sabrina. Keith and Amy married one year later. Keith was not quite 20 years old.

The two events — his father's death and the birth of his daughter — forced Keith to take stock of his life. He set firm priorities for himself. Most important were God and family. School came next. Keith was majoring in sociology and he was determined to get his degree.

Basketball came last. Still, after a great junior season, Keith considered leaving school early for the NBA. That season, he scored 21.4 points and grabbed 8.8 rebounds per game. Experts predicted he would be chosen among the top 15 players in the NBA draft and could get a multimillion-dollar contract. Keith saw that he would be able to fulfill his dream of playing pro basketball *and* take care of his family.

The opportunity was tempting. But Keith had promised his father that he would earn his college degree. Besides, he thought about the example he would be setting for his own children. "I can't tell my kids to go to college if I haven't completed it myself," he said.

So Keith returned to Utah. He blossomed, averaging 22 points and 9.5 rebounds per game as a senior. He was named the WAC Player of the Year for a record third time. During the WAC tournament, he sank last-second shots twice to carry Utah to the conference title. Keith ended his college career as the top scorer in WAC history (2,542 points). Utah retired his uniform number, 44.

Learning the game
★★★★★★★★★★★

That June, the Philadelphia 76ers made Keith the number two pick overall in the 1997 NBA draft, after Tim Duncan. Hours later, the New Jersey Nets acquired Keith in a trade. The Nets had had 20 losing seasons in the previous 30 years. They hadn't had a superstar player since the legendary Julius "Dr. J" Erving, in the 1970's. The Nets' coach, John Calipari, was convinced that Keith could lead the Nets back to the playoffs. So he landed him as part of a big eight-player trade.

Keith got off to a slow start with the Nets. He sprained his right ankle in the pre-season, and missed the team's first 17 games. He could have gotten down about not being able to play. Instead, he turned it into a learning experience.

After each game, he sought out Jayson Williams, the Nets' All-Star center. (Jayson is not related to Sacramento's Jason Williams.) Said Jayson, "Keith's always asking me, 'How do you rebound? How do you do this? How do you do that?'"

Watching from the bench, Keith studied each of his teammates. He learned how every one moved without the

---

Keith's Hall of Fame Double

There's a lot of Larry Bird's game in Keith Van Horn. Larry was a Hall of Fame forward who led the Boston Celtics to three NBA titles in the 1980's. He became head coach of the Indiana Pacers in 1997. Like Larry, Keith is a clutch shooter who can score from anywhere. Like Larry, too, he has a sweet jump shot and a passion to win. Keith is faster than Larry was, and a better leaper, but Larry was a better passer and had extraordinary court vision.

---

ball. He learned their favorite shooting spots on the court. As a result, he was able to fit in quickly when he finally started playing.

In Keith's first NBA game, against the Philadelphia 76ers, he scored 11 points. Then he went on a tear. He led the team in scoring in eight of its next 12 games. His biggest moment came in the final game of the 1997-98 regular season, when he led New Jersey past the Detroit Pistons, 114–101. Keith's 25 points helped clinch the Nets' first playoff berth in four years!

New Jersey faced the eventual NBA champions, the Chicago Bulls, in the opening round of the playoffs. The Bulls eliminated them in three hard-fought games. Keith had the flu and couldn't contribute much. Yet the Bulls were impressed. Michael Jordan predicted big things for Keith and the Nets the following season.

The Nets' new leader
★★★★★★★★★★★

But the 1998-99 season was a disappointment for the Nets. They were hurt badly by injuries. Keith missed eight games with a fractured left thumb. Still, he finished the season as the fifth-leading scorer in the NBA, with 21.8 points per game. But the Nets finished in last place in the Atlantic Division, with a 16–34 record.

It would have been easy for Keith to toss in the towel after that, wait for free agency, and sign with a top team. But that would have been out of character. All his life, both on the court and off, Keith has prided himself on being a leader, on accepting responsibility. He wanted to help make the Nets champions. So he signed a new, long-term contract extension with the team after the season.

"We're a young team with a lot of guys who are going to be here awhile," he said afterward. He mentioned his team-mates: Jayson, swingman Kendall Gill, and star guards Kerry Kittles and Stephon Marbury. "Hopefully, we can keep this team together and do some great things."

Knowing Keith, he'll make certain they will.

JASON KIDD

He's one team leader who would rather pass than score
★★★★★★★★★★★

Jason Kidd of the Phoenix Suns is a giver. Watch him when he is dribbling upcourt. He is happiest when he spots an open teammate. That means he can pass the ball to him and set up a basket. In fact, Jason is so unselfish that, unlike many of today's point guards, he would *rather* pass than shoot.

Consider this play in a May 1999 game against the Houston Rockets: Jason was driving toward the basket. He faked a shot, forcing Houston center Hakeem Olajuwon to leave the basket to guard him. Instead of shooting, though, Jason flicked a no-look, over-the-shoulder pass to teammate Clifford Robinson. With Hakeem out of position, Clifford was able to drive to the hoop for a one-handed slam.

"I enjoy when a teammate scores," Jason said afterward. "I always feel part of me scored the basket."

Jason built his
reputation as a
passer, but the
man knows how
to score, too.

RISING

Jason's style of play reminds people of the two best point guards ever: Hall of Famer Bob Cousy of the Boston Celtics and John Stockton of the Utah Jazz. Bob helped the Celtics win six NBA titles from 1957 to 1963 with his ball-handling skills and pinpoint passes. John set NBA records for assists and helped make the Jazz one of the top teams of the 1990's.

But Bob and John were more than unselfish givers. They were team leaders. And that combination is what made them truly great. Jason would be the first to tell you that he is not a born leader. "I had to learn through trial and error," he said. What he might not tell you — but which is also true — is that during the 1998-99 season, Jason became a leader.

Shy — except at sports
★★★★★★★★★★★

Jason was born March 23, 1973, in San Francisco, California. He grew up in nearby Oakland Hills, California, with his two younger sisters and his parents. Jason's father, Steve, was an airline ticket agent. His mother, Anne, worked at a bank. Each worked for the same company for more than 30 years. "That taught me a lot about hard work, commitment, and never quitting or giving up," Jason said. "I also got my unselfish nature from them, which they got from growing up in large families."

Jason was shy, except when it came to sports. He was the only third-grader to volunteer for the fourth-grade basketball team. Basketball soon became Jason's favorite sport. He modeled his game after Magic Johnson, the great Los Angeles

Laker point guard known for his flashy, between-the-legs and behind-the-head passes. Jason practiced alone for hours at a time, imagining he was defending against Magic.

By age 12, Jason was bugging teenagers at the local playground to let him play in their pickup games. At first they refused. They said he was too young. But Jason promised that he would pass the ball instead of taking shots. The older kids liked that idea because they wanted to score.

Once on the court, Jason unveiled all the slick moves he had been practicing on his own. On offense, his passes were so quick and unexpected, his teammates often weren't ready for them. On defense, Jason hounded the ball handler until he could steal the ball. Soon, Jason was welcome to the older kids' game. "Unselfishness goes a long way," he said.

High school superstar
★★★★★★★★★★★

When Jason enrolled at St. Joseph of Notre Dame High School, in nearby Alameda, California, in 1988, he was already 6-foot-2. He dominated his team and the league. Jason averaged 12.1 points, 8.5 assists, and 9 rebounds per game. He was named California's Freshman Player of the Year. Jason's ball-handling skills were so good that St. Joseph coach Frank played him at point guard, even though he was taller and stronger than many of his teammates.

As a sophomore, Jason did even better. He averaged 19 points, 9.4 assists, and 8.6 rebounds per game and was

RISING

STAT CITY
JASON FREDERICK KIDD

★**Team:** Phoenix Suns   ★**Position:** Guard

★**Acquired:** Drafted No. 2 overall by Dallas in 1994, traded to Phoenix in 1996

★**Born:** March 23, 1973, in San Francisco, California

★**Height:** 6-foot-4   ★**Weight:** 212 pounds

★**College:** University of California at Berkeley

★**Career Bests:** 38 points (against Houston, 4-11-95), 25 assists (against Utah, 2-8-96), 6 steals (nine times)

★**Honors:** 1998-99 All-NBA First Team, 1998-99 NBA All-Defensive First Team, 1994-95 co-NBA Rookie of the Year

★**Personal:** Married to Joumana Samaha; has two sons, Trey and Jason, Junior; listens to Chante Moore

named California Player of the Year. In his junior year, he led the school to its first state basketball title, and he was named a *Parade* magazine High School All-America.

By Jason's senior year, crowds at St. Joseph's home games were so large, some games had to be moved to the huge Oakland Coliseum! The school sold "Jason Kidd" T-shirts and posters. Jason was mobbed for autographs after every game. He led St. Joseph to its second state title, averaging 25.3 points, 9.6 assists, and 7.4 rebounds per game.

Jason was named the Naismith National Prep Player of the Year. His 719 career steals set a national high school record.

Jason could have gone to almost any top college basketball program in the country. But he chose the University of California at Berkeley because it was close to his Oakland home. In 1992-93, his freshman season, Jason led Cal to a 21–9 record — its best mark in 33 years! He led the entire Pacific Athletic Conference in assists (222) and all major colleges in steals (3.8 per game). Then, in the NCAA tournament, he scored the go-ahead basket that gave Cal a stunning 82–77 victory over heavily favored Duke.

Jason improved in his sophomore season. He led all major colleges in assists, with 9.1 per game. He took Cal back to the NCAA tournament and was named a First Team All-America. After the season, Jason felt he had learned all he could at the college level. He entered the 1994 NBA draft.

The Three J's
★★★★★★★★★★★

The Dallas Mavericks selected Jason number two overall, after forward Glenn Robinson of the Milwaukee Bucks. Dallas was a struggling franchise. Jason hoped to change that.

Jason was one of three top young players who were expected to someday lead Dallas to the playoffs. The others were guard Jim Jackson and forward Jamal Mashburn. Jim, Jamal, and Jason were nicknamed the Three J's. Jason's passing helped Jim and Jamal improve their scoring

Jason's Hall of Fame Double

Jason reminds older fans of Hall of Fame point guard Bob Cousy. Bob played with the Boston Celtics from 1950 to 1963. Like Jason, Bob was the flashiest ball handler of his day. Bob was nicknamed Houdini of the Hardwood, after the famous magician Harry Houdini, for his behind-the-back passes. Like Jason, Bob led the NBA in assists. But Bob did it for eight straight seasons and helped lead the Celtics to six NBA titles!

averages. Each of them had a 50-point game during the season! Jason averaged 11.7 points, 7.7 assists, and 5.4 rebounds per game, and shared Rookie of the Year honors with Detroit Piston star Grant Hill. Best of all, the Mavs won 23 more games than they had won the season before! Things were looking up.

Dallas began the 1995-96 season by winning five of its first six games. Jason began to dream about leading Dallas to its first-ever playoffs. But then the Three J's started bickering. They argued over who should be handling the ball, who should get the most shots, and who should be the team leader. The team started losing.

Jason thinks that if he had known more about being a leader, he might have been able to help the Three J's to work out their problems and focus on winning. As the point guard, he was supposed to be the floor boss. But, said

Jason, "I didn't know how to get the team to respond to me."

Dallas managed just 26 wins — 10 fewer than the previous season. Jason finished the season averaging 16.6 points, 9.7 assists, and 6.8 rebounds per game, and was named to the NBA All-Star team. But he wasn't pleased.

Jason realized that his personal stats hadn't helped the Mavericks. Selflessness was fine, but the team needed leadership, and he wasn't giving it. Jason felt frustrated. "It's not my nature to say things or get into people's faces or confront them," he said.

Professor Johnson
★★★★★★★★★★★

Things were no better the following season. The Three J's continued to feud, and Dallas kept losing. Finally, on December 26, 1996, the team lost patience and traded Jason. He went to the Phoenix Suns in exchange for three players.

Jason got off to a bad start with Phoenix. He hurt his collarbone in his very first game and missed the next 21 games. He decided to use that time as a chance to learn.

The Suns were a strong, smart, veteran team. They already had a great point guard in Kevin Johnson. Kevin was in his 10th NBA season, and had played in three All-Star Games. Jason watched Kevin and listened. "Kevin talked about what was needed to be done to win and what needed to be said to motivate players," Jason said. "I learned that I needed to be more vocal."

RISING

Jason joined Kevin in Phoenix's backcourt after his collarbone healed. Kevin was the point guard and the leader, and Rex Chapman and Jason were the shooting guards. Together, they led the Suns to the playoffs. For the season, Kevin ranked third in the NBA in assists, with 9.3 per game, and Jason ranked fourth, with 9 per game.

Learning to lead
★★★★★★★★★★★

n 1997-98, Jason took control of the Suns' offense. Kevin became *his* backup. Jason tried to put Kevin's lessons into action. He spoke up in the locker room when he felt his teammates were losing focus. It wasn't as hard to do as he had once thought. "It's just a matter of picking your spots about when to say stuff," he said.

Jason finished the 1997-98 season averaging 9.1 assists per game, second-best in the NBA. He helped lead Phoenix to a 56–26 record and a playoff spot. In 1998-99, Jason became the first Phoenix player ever to lead the NBA in assists, with 10.8 per game. He also averaged 16.9 points per game. Again, he helped lead the Suns to the playoffs.

Kevin retired after the 1998-99 season, after two seasons as Jason's on-court teacher. By then, Jason was ready to take charge. Jason's new confidence in being a leader, he said, "has really taken my game to another level."

Jason the Giver is now giving his teammates more than the ball. He's giving them leadership, focus, and — Suns fans hope — victory!

JASON WILLIAMS

Man of a thousand moves

★★★★★★★★★★★★

Jason Williams likes to figure out his jaw-dropping basketball moves in advance. The Sacramento Kings' star guard then waits for an opportunity to use them in an NBA game.

Here's one that Jason has practiced for quite awhile: He'll race upcourt, the ball seemingly glued to his hand. Teammates will be sprinting down each sideline. In front of him will be a line of defenders. Jason will cup the ball in his left hand and take it behind his back. But instead of passing with his left hand, he will suddenly whip his right *elbow* behind his back and bat the ball to a teammate for an easy layup. In the stands, 15,000 fans will leap to their feet in delight — and disbelief.

Jason has already tried out the move on the Orlando Magic's Nick Anderson in summer pickup games in Orlando, Florida. Former Sacramento teammate Vernon

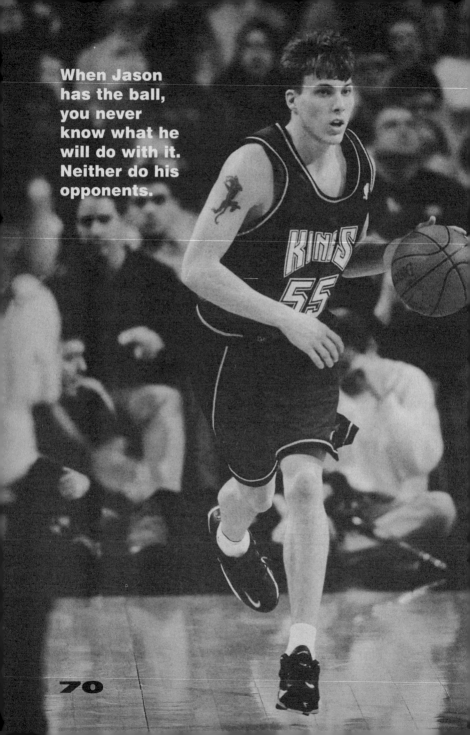

When Jason
has the ball,
you never
know what he
will do with it.
Neither do his
opponents.

Maxwell has seen the move, too, during Kings practices.

If Jason goes public with it, it's sure to end up an ESPN *SportsCenter* highlight. He makes highlight-worthy plays almost nightly. Perhaps it will be replayed as often as his memorable move against Gary Payton of the Seattle SuperSonics in 1999. Gary is the NBA's best defensive guard, and Jason stopped him cold by taking a hesitation step, switching hands, then gliding past him for a layup.

There is only one other player in basketball history who made as many acrobatic plays as Jason does. That was "Pistol Pete" Maravich, the 1970's Hall of Fame guard who was named one of the 50 greatest players in NBA history (*see box, page 76*).

"I'm just astonished at Jason," Sacramento teammate Chris Webber said.

Even more astonishing than Jason's moves, though, is how close he came to throwing his talent away.

Alone in the gym
★★★★★★★★★★★

Jason was born November 18, 1975, in Belle, West Virginia. Belle is a depressed factory town of 2,500 people. Jason was a reluctant student who excelled at sports. He was the captain and quarterback of his junior high football team. One of his teammates was his buddy Randy Moss, now a star receiver for the NFL's Minnesota Vikings. Jason was close to his mother, Delana, and his older brother, Shawn. But he was especially

RISING

devoted to his father, Terry, a West Virginia state trooper.

The Williams family lived in a house smack in the middle of Belle's DuPont High School campus. They lived there because of a security arrangement the school had made with Jason's dad. It came in handy: The gym was 100 yards away from the Williams's house, and Dad had a key! Jason spent as much time there as he could.

After age 15, Jason practically lived at the gym. His parents went through a bitter divorce, and Jason took it hard. Basketball had always been his favorite sport. Now it became his refuge, a safe place away from his troubles. He would spend hour after hour in the gym, practicing alone.

Often, Jason wouldn't even shoot the ball. Instead, he would work on his dribbling technique. To make it harder to handle the ball, he would wear leather gloves and wrap weights around his wrists. Then he would throw behind-the-back passes toward a two-foot square he had drawn on a cinder-block wall.

Switching schools
★★★★★★★★★★★

Each winter, when hoops season rolled around, Jason's hard work paid off. During his senior year, in 1993-94, Jason and Randy led DuPont High to the West Virginia state championship game. Though DuPont lost, 79–73, Jason had a tournament-record 13 assists.

Jason seemed headed for a spectacular college career. But his college years were as rocky as his home life. At first, he accepted a scholarship to Providence College, in Rhode Island. But he backed out when the Providence head coach resigned to take another job. Next, Jason enrolled at Fork Union Military Academy, in Virginia. But he didn't like military-school life, and lasted less than a week.

Then, in spring, 1995, Jason landed at West Virginia's Marshall University. He had to sit out his first season because of NCAA rules about transferring from one college to another. When he finally got to play, in the 1995-96 season, Jason quickly made his mark. The point guard dazzled teammates and opponents alike with his behind-

STAT CITY
JASON CHANDLER WILLIAMS

★**Team:** Sacramento Kings   ★**Position:** Guard

★**Acquired:** Drafted No. 7 overall by Sacramento, in 1998

★**Born:** November 18, 1975, in Belle, West Virginia

★**Height:** 6-foot-1   ★**Weight:** 190 pounds

★**College:** University of Florida

★**Career Bests:** 27 points (against Minnesota, 4-23-99), 14 assists (against L.A. Clippers, 4-19-99)

★**Honors:** 1999 All-Rookie First Team

★**Personal:** Single; listens to Master P; favorite actor is Bruce Willis

the-back passes, over-the-shoulder passes, and a dozen other hard-to-believe moves. Jason averaged 6.4 assists per game to lead the Southern Conference as a freshman. He also averaged 13.4 points per game.

In and out of trouble
★★★★★★★★★★★

After the season, Marshall coach Billy Donovan left to become head coach at the University of Florida. Jason liked the coach and decided to follow him. Transferring meant that Jason had to sit out the 1996-97 season. Midway through it, he grew so frustrated, he called his father to say he was quitting school.

"Jason came home, and he sat here in this house for three weeks," his father said. "He didn't do anything. We have a little 7-Eleven down here on the corner, and that's where a lot of the guys who used to play sports hang around. We call it the All-7-Eleven Team. I said to Jason, 'What are you gonna do, be All-7-Eleven?' "

Jason realized he had made a mistake and returned to school. Coach Donovan was still angry with him for quitting, but he let Jason back on the team.

But Jason's troubles weren't over. Twice he was suspended in the 1997-98 season for violating team rules. Once, Jason tested positive for marijuana. A second time, Coach Donovan didn't like the way Jason had sulked on the bench during losses. Each suspension lasted one game.

After the second suspension, Coach Donovan agreed

to give Jason one last chance. In a game against the University of Kentucky, Jason showed his thanks. He led Florida to an 86–78 upset win over the Wildcats, who would go on to win the national championship. Jason completely dominated the game. He scored 24 points, including four 3-pointers, grabbed six rebounds, and showed off some amazing moves.

Florida went 12–8 with Jason in the lineup. He was leading the Southeastern Conference in assists (6.7 per game) and steals (2.7 per game) while scoring 17.1 points per game. He was the hottest new college star in the country!

Then, as quickly as Jason had emerged, he was gone. On February 17, 1998, Coach Donovan suspended him for the rest of the season. Jason had tested positive for marijuana a second time.

"He knew the consequences if he tested positive again," Coach Donovan said. "And that's the thing that was disappointing to me: He knew the consequences and did it anyway." Coach Donovan felt betrayed.

Starting over
★★★★★★★★★★★

Jason's career at Florida was over. His chance to be a top NBA draft pick seemed slim, too. Pro teams shy away from drug users. And since Jason had never taken school seriously, he didn't have much hope of getting a decent job outside of basketball. It looked as if Jason was headed for the All-7-Eleven Team in Belle.

Jason's father, the state trooper, said, "I'm embarrassed."

Jason finally realized how dumb he had been. He was close to losing everything he had worked for. And for what? The short-lived high of marijuana? Jason decided to clean up his act. He quit using drugs and admitted that he needed to grow up.

Jason couldn't return to the University of Florida, so he applied for early entry into the 1998 NBA draft. He might have been a top three pick. But because of his history of drug use, experts predicted that he would slip much lower. Once again, Coach Donovan stepped in to help.

Jason's Hall of Fame Double

Jason looks and plays like Hall of Fame guard "Pistol Pete" Maravich, who played for three NBA teams from 1970 through 1980. Jason wears his hair in a mop top, as Pete did. He has Pete's lean build, and on the court, he has the same swagger and self-confidence. The two are perhaps the greatest ball handlers in NBA history.

"I could have told all the NBA general managers that this kid was not worth the trouble," Coach Donovan said. "But I told them he was a good kid who made poor choices. A little quiet, tough to get to know, needs to grow up."

On June 24, 1998, the Sacramento Kings made Jason the number seven pick overall. Was he lucky! Jason has behaved himself ever since.

In his NBA debut, against the San Antonio Spurs, Jason made 21 points, 5 steals, 4 rebounds, and a dozen eye-popping moves. Afterward, Spur guard Avery Johnson declared: "That rookie almost put me in retirement."

Later in the season, against the Washington Wizards, he flipped the ball behind his back to his opposite hand, then sank the shot with that hand. In Vancouver, while lying on the floor, he flipped the ball blindly over his shoulder to a teammate under the basket for a score!

Where do those amazing moves come from? "I just play by instinct," Jason said.

Court magician
★★★★★★★★★★

Thanks to the flashy rookie, the surprising Kings made the playoffs. Jason averaged 12.8 points, 6 assists, and 1.9 steals per game. He also made 100 3-point field goals, the fourth-highest total among all NBA players. He finished second to Vince Carter for the NBA's 1999 Rookie of the Year award.

"I think our league needs players like him," Sacramento coach Rick Adelman said afterward. "Our game gets pretty stagnant sometimes. People respond to a little guy out there, showing all those moves. The game is not all dunks. I'm having fun watching him play."

Even his opponents are paying close attention. Jason has them all wondering what magic he will perform next.

"Just keep watching," he said. As if anyone could stop.

SHAREEF ABDUR-RAHIM

The best young star you've never heard of
★★★★★★★★★★★

The quiet man. That's a fitting nickname for Shareef Abdur-Rahim. The 6-foot-9 forward is a low-key player. He performs out of the spotlight, playing for the Vancouver Grizzlies way up in western Canada.

Perhaps that's why the quiet man is overlooked when NBA honors are passed out. Shareef entered the league in 1996, and based on the stats, he deserved to be the 1997 NBA Rookie of the Year. He came in third. The next season, he probably should have been named an All-Star. It didn't happen. Shareef is the kind of player who All-Star voters gush over after seeing him play. But when it comes time for these voters to actually vote, there's no screaming headline or sneaker ad to remind them of the high-flying Vancouver star.

The lack of recognition doesn't bother Shareef. "I don't

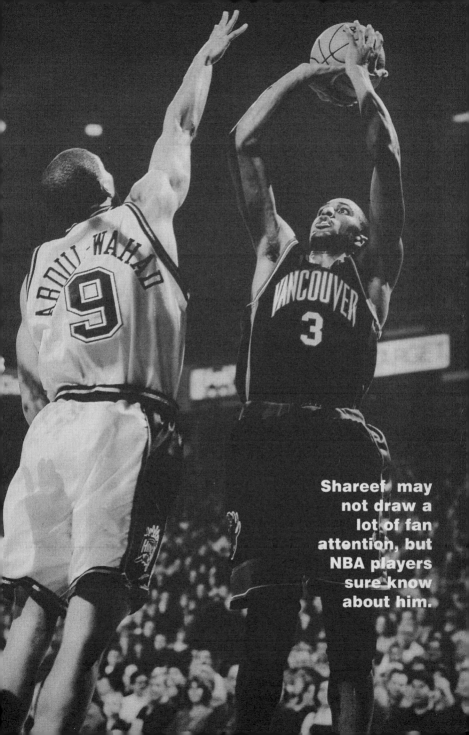

Shareef may
not draw a
lot of fan
attention, but
NBA players
sure know
about him.

play basketball for that," he said. "I just want to know that I came as close as I could to fulfilling my potential."

How's this for fulfilling potential? During the 1998-99 season, Shareef averaged 23 points per game to finish fourth in the NBA in scoring. He also averaged 7.5 rebounds and 3.4 assists per game.

"Everyone talks about Kobe Bryant and Kevin Garnett being so young and talented," said Vin Baker of the Seattle SuperSonics. "Shareef is either better or at least at the same level. He just doesn't get the hype they do."

It's too bad, because in a world in which many athletes are self-centered and filled with arrogance, Shareef is like a whiff of fresh air.

Like father, like son
★★★★★★★★★★★

hareef was born December 11, 1976, in Marietta, Georgia. He is the second-oldest of eight children. Shareef was very mature, even as a toddler. His mother, Aminah, recalls him saying something when he was 2 years old that was so profound, she told her husband, William, "Even grown men don't think that way!"

By age 6, religion had become a major part of Shareef's life. His father is an imam, or Muslim spiritual leader. (Muslims are followers of the religion of Islam.) Shareef became a Muslim, too. He still is. It gives him a sense of purpose. Shareef prays five times a day. When praying, Muslims face Mecca, Saudi Arabia, the holiest of Muslim cities.

Shareef travels all over with the Grizzlies, so he uses a compass to locate the direction of Mecca wherever he is. During Ramadan, a month-long holy celebration that starts in mid-January, he fasts (does not eat) from sunrise to sunset.

"It is not compulsory for children to fast," his father said. "But to give you an idea of the kind of person Shareef is, he asked to join in the fasting when he was six. Now he looks forward to it, like an old friend coming to visit."

STAT CITY
SHAREEF ABDUR-RAHIM

★**Nickname:** Reef

★**Team:** Vancouver Grizzlies   ★**Position:** Forward

★**Acquired:** Drafted No. 3 overall by Vancouver in 1996

★**Born:** December 11, 1976, in Marietta, Georgia

★**Height:** 6-foot-9   ★**Weight:** 230 pounds

★**College:** University of California at Berkeley

★**Career Bests:** 39 points (against Boston, 2-17-99),

17 rebounds (twice), 13 assists (against Houston, 2-14-97)

★**Honors:** 1996-97 NBA All-Rookie First Team,

1995-96 AP Third Team All-America

★**Personal:** Single, first name means "Noble" in Arabic,

last name means "servant of the most merciful one."

RISING

Shareef also began playing basketball at age 6. When Shareef brought home a flyer announcing a recreational basketball league, his father signed him up and then helped him with his game. His father had been an athlete himself. As a young man, he had two NFL tryouts.

William made Shareef practice ball handling with a tennis ball. After that, dribbling a basketball seemed easy! William coached Shareef's fourth-grade team. He remembers the day when, out of nowhere, Shareef did a perfect spin move while driving to the basket.

"At that age, we were just teaching the basics," William said. "Lo and behold, he has the guts to try this in the game!" No one knew that Shareef had been cooking up that move on his own, spending hours in the driveway with a basketball.

Mr. Georgia Basketball
★★★★★★★★★★★★

Shareef wasn't afraid of hard work. He applied his sense of purpose to all that he did. At 14, Shareef walked two miles for a job interview at a fast-food restaurant. The manager, impressed that he had gone to such lengths, hired him on the spot.

That was a tough year for Shareef. His parents divorced. He moved in with his mother, but stayed close to his dad.

To top it off, Shareef was cut from his high school team as a freshman. But by his junior year, he was good enough to lead unranked Wheeler High to its first-ever Georgia state title. In the championship game, he scored 26 points, 10 of them in the final quarter. He also had nine rebounds and seven blocked shots. Shareef shared Mr. Georgia Basketball honors with Matt Hapring, who later played for the NBA's Orlando Magic.

A busy summer followed. Shareef played for a U.S. national team in a qualifying tournament for the 1995 World Junior Basketball Championship. He averaged 16.8 points and 10.1 rebounds per game!

When Shareef returned to Wheeler High for his senior season, he was almost unstoppable. He led the team to 23 straight victories before Wheeler lost in the state final.

Vancouver's first true star
★★★★★★★★★★★

Shareef could have gone to almost any college he chose. He picked the University of California at Berkeley because the school had a solid community of Muslim students. Shareef became an instant star. In his first three college games, he scored 33, 29, and 32 points! Coach Bob Bender of the University of Washington called him "as good a freshman as I've seen — ever." Shareef's quickness and his ability to find cracks in the other team's defense made him extremely tough to defend.

In one game, against the University of Southern California, Shareef scored 28 points and grabbed 13 rebounds to rally Cal to a 63–60 come-from-behind win. "Poor guy probably hurt his back, carrying us all night," said teammate Randy Duck. That season, 1995-96, Shareef became the first freshman in the history of the Pacific-10 Conference to be named conference Player of the Year.

Todd Bozeman was Cal's coach. After Shareef's freshman season, Coach Bozeman resigned from Cal. Partly because of that and partly because he felt he was ready for the NBA, Shareef decided to leave college and enter the 1996 draft. Vancouver made him the number three pick overall, behind Allen Iverson and Marcus Camby.

Shareef's Hall of Fame Double

Older fans watch Shareef slicing upcourt to the basket, and they think of James Worthy. James played for the Los Angeles Lakers from 1982 to 1994 and helped them win three NBA titles. He was selected as one of the 50 greatest players in NBA history. Like James, Shareef isn't overpowering under the basket. Instead, he darts and jukes through the lane, opening a hole to the hoop that few players could imagine.

Shareef didn't get off to a fast start in the NBA, but he improved steadily as the season went on. He averaged 11.5 points per game in the month of November, 18.9 points in December, 20 points in January, and 24.5 points in February. For the season, he averaged 18.7 points and 6.9 rebounds a game. He finished third in Rookie of the Year voting, behind Allen Iverson and Stephon Marbury.

Shareef was especially effective under the basket, where

his athletic ability allowed him to shine. "He can score in traffic, which a lot of players have trouble with," said Vancouver coach Brian Hill. "He can hang in the air and take contact. And because he's a little unorthodox, he's able to score while he's drawing fouls." Coach Hill considered Shareef the most talented rookie he ever worked with — and he coached Shaquille O'Neal and Penny Hardaway when *they* were rookies with the Orlando Magic!

Learning to be a leader
★★★★★★★★★★★

Shareef didn't rest on his accomplishments. Instead, he worked even harder at his game over the summer. Together with All-Star guard Gary Payton of the Seattle SuperSonics, he worked out every day in an Oakland, California, gym.

In July, Shareef went to Europe with a team of NBA stars. Several older players took him under their wings. "He spent a lot of time with me and Scottie [Pippen], asking what it takes to win and be a leader," said Charles Barkley, who had entered the NBA in 1984. "I told him, 'Number one, you have to go out there and kick butt every night. But you have to accept the fact that it's a big responsibility to be a star. You have to lead by example, to make sure that other players play hard.' "

The experience on tour had a strong effect on Shareef. "I try to draw from all the great players," he said. "I watch teams like the Utah Jazz. They aren't very exciting, but they do all the little things right. That's why they're so good."

Shareef's willingness to study, combined with his off-season workouts, paid off in the 1997-98 season. He averaged 22.3 points per game, sixth-best in the league. He scored in double figures in 81 of the Grizzlies' 82 games! Despite Shareef's play, though, Vancouver finished with a 19–63 record. Most nights, the young team was overmatched.

The hard work isn't over
★★★★★★★★★★★★

Shareef could have become frustrated. He could have waited to become a free agent and then signed with a winning team. But that's not the way he is. He was taught by his parents, and educated through his religion, that good things come from hard work. So, after the 1997-98 season, he signed a six-year contract extension with the Grizzlies. He wants to lead them to the title, just as Michael Jordan led the Chicago Bulls to the top of the NBA.

Things started to look up. In the 1998 draft, the Grizzlies landed two top prospects: guards Mike Bibby and Felipe Lopez. And Shareef continued to improve. In 1998-99, he finished fourth in the league in scoring. He also had career bests in other key statistics, with averages of 7.5 rebounds, 3.4 assists, and 1.38 steals per game.

"I want to win," Shareef said. "I want to be as good as I can be. I don't want to leave the game and look back, thinking I could have done something more."

Knowing him, that's not possible.

KEVIN GARNETT

He changed how big men play the game

★★★★★★★★★★★

Kevin Garnett is a kind, playful, fun-loving guy who is devoted to his family and to his friends from childhood. He listens to Whitney Houston. His favorite book is F. Scott Fitzgerald's classic novel *The Great Gatsby*. In his spare time, he takes business courses through a University of Minnesota correspondence-school program. In short, Kevin is pretty much a regular guy — until he picks up a basketball.

Then he transforms himself into a basketball revolutionary. He has changed the way his position — forward — is played. Before Kevin joined the Minnesota Timberwolves, in 1995, the classic NBA big man stayed close to the basket on defense and didn't do much ball handling on offense. But Kevin, who says he is 6-foot-11 (others, including his coach, believe he is taller), does it all.

"Here's a 7-foot-1 small forward who can shoot the ball,

Kevin is like an octopus on defense. Under the basket, he is all arms and elbows.

handle the ball like a guard, rebound like a center, and play defense like a power forward," said Wolves coach Phil "Flip" Saunders. "Before he's through, he may be the most versatile player ever."

That's a big part of why Kevin was the first player in more than 20 years to successfully jump from high school directly to the NBA. And why, three years later, the Wolves signed him to the richest contract in sports history. Kevin has come a long way from his poor South Carolina beginnings.

So tall so fast
★★★★★★★★★★★

evin was born May 19, 1976, in Greenville, South Carolina. His mother, Shirley, was a factory worker who earned extra money working as a hairstylist.

Kevin was 12 when he moved with his mother, stepfather, and sisters, Sonya and Ashley, to nearby Mauldin, South Carolina. By then, Kevin was obsessed with basketball. "Every time you saw him, he had a ball," his childhood friend Baron "Bear" Frank, said. "Sun up. Sun down. Up and down the street, all day long."

By age 12, Kevin was already 5-foot-10. But he wasn't a good player. He was growing so rapidly, his coordination couldn't keep pace. Bear remembers that when Kevin was 6-foot-6 and in high school, he still couldn't dunk. In pickup games, the neighborhood kids beat him easily.

But Kevin kept working at the game. His family didn't have much, and he used basketball as his escape. He would watch tapes of his favorite player, Magic Johnson, who starred for the Los Angeles Lakers from 1979 to 1991, and try to copy his moves. People would sometimes spot Kevin alone in a local park, shooting baskets after midnight.

Moving to Chicago
★★★★★★★★★★★

Kevin's mother disapproved of his spending so much time playing ball. She wanted him to concentrate on his schoolwork. Kevin didn't tell his mother he had made the Mauldin High School team until after the season began. He was afraid she would make him quit. But she let him play.

By Kevin's junior year in high school, he was 6-foot-7 and had at last grown into his lanky body. The change in his ability was amazing. That season, 1993-94, he averaged 27 points, 17 rebounds, and 7 blocked shots per game while leading Mauldin High to a 22–7 record. His basketball future seemed bright.

Then an off-court incident almost ended Kevin's hoop dreams. There was a fight at school. A white student was badly injured. Though Kevin and others insisted that Kevin wasn't involved, he was among those arrested. The charges were later dropped and Kevin was cleared completely, but his mother decided that it would be best if he went to another school.

By then, Kevin was set on playing pro ball. His mother remembered William Nelson, a coach that Kevin had met at a summer-league all-star camp. Coach Nelson coached at Farragut Academy, a private high school in Chicago, Illinois. Kevin's mother spoke to Coach Nelson and then moved her family to Chicago so that Kevin could go to Farragut.

For Kevin's family, life in Chicago was difficult. They didn't know anyone, and Kevin's mother had a hard time finding work. Many nights, they ate only rice for dinner. But the family was determined to succeed.

Kevin grew another few inches, to 6-foot-11, in his senior year. He ran the offense like a quick-footed guard, dashing everywhere on the court. But he also scored, rebounded, and had quick hands. No one could stop him! Kevin averaged 26 points, 18 rebounds, 7 assists, and 6 blocked shots per game.

Kevin led Farragut to a 28–2 record and the state tournament quarterfinals. He was named Illinois's Mr. Basketball. "He is absolutely the most complete player I've seen in my whole life," Coach Nelson said. "I've never seen any player who is basically seven feet tall with all those skills."

From high school to the NBA
★★★★★★★★★★★

Kevin wanted to attend college. His first choice was the University of Michigan. But his college-entrance exam score was too low. So he took the test again. But he also declared himself eligible for the 1995 NBA draft, in case his exam score was still not high enough.

To most people, jumping straight from high school to the NBA seemed a long shot. Only three players had ever done

RISING

STAT CITY
KEVIN MAURICE GARNETT

★**Nickname:** K.G.

★**Team:** Minnesota Timberwolves ★**Position:** Forward

★**Acquired:** Drafted No. 5 overall by Minnesota, in 1995

★**Born:** May 19, 1976, in Greenville, South Carolina

★**Height:** 6-foot-11 ★**Weight:** 220 pounds

★**High School:** Farragut Academy (Chicago, Illinois)

★**Career Bests:** 33 points (twice), 20 rebounds (against Washington, 11-13-97)

★**Honors:** Member, 2000 U.S. Olympic Men's Basketball Team; 1998-99 All-NBA third team; NBA All-Star, 1997, 1998

★**Personal:** Single; listens to Whitney Houston; loves video games

it successfully, none of them in the last 20 years. Some NBA teams were invited to watch Kevin in a special workout. They were amazed by what they saw.

Kevin McHale, now Minnesota's vice president of basketball operations, and Flip Saunders, who was then a Wolves assistant coach, were two of those who attended. They were struck not only by Kevin's athletic skill, but also by his maturity. "When you talk to him," Coach Saunders said, "Kevin looks you right in the eye. You can see his focus, his concentration. He was going to absorb everything that we taught him."

Hours before the 1995 NBA draft, Kevin learned that he had scored high enough on his last college entrance exam to play at Michigan! By then, though, he had made his mind up to turn pro. Minnesota made him the fifth pick overall.

Making the playoffs
★★★★★★★★★★★

Bill Blair, who was the Wolves' coach at the time, was instantly impressed by Kevin. But the coach worried about rushing him. So he limited Kevin's court time. Then in mid-December, Coach Blair was replaced by Coach Saunders. Within weeks, Kevin was a starter. For the rest of the season, Kevin averaged 14 points, 8.4 rebounds, and 2 blocks per game. He also earned everybody's notice — even Michael Jordan's.

"If his game continues to grow, he'll be an All-Star in two years," Michael said. Michael was wrong. It took Kevin just *one* year to make the All-Star team.

Kevin could have let his new stardom go to his head. Instead, he remained the same person he had always been. He bought a house in a quiet Minneapolis, Minnesota, suburb. He put a basketball hoop in the driveway and a trampoline in his backyard. He invited his sister, Ashley, and a friend from Mauldin High, Jamie "Bug" Peters, to move in with him. And he kept working hard at his game.

Kevin improved dramatically in 1996-97, his second NBA

season. On offense, he averaged 17 points, 8 rebounds, and 3.1 assists per game. But he was named an All-Star because of his defense. "He comes out of nowhere," Tom Gugliotta, a teammate at the time, said of Kevin's defense. "Sometimes, he might be ten feet away from you when you go up to shoot, and then suddenly he's three feet over your head."

Kevin and Tom had taken a last place Wolves team and made it better. When the Wolves added point guard Stephon Marbury in 1996, the team reached the playoffs for the first time in franchise history. Even though the Wolves lost in three games to the Houston Rockets, people began to view them as a team with potential.

A really big star
★★★★★★★★★★★

That off-season, the Wolves signed Kevin to a six-year, $126 million contract, the biggest in sports history. Some worried that all that money would change Kevin. But if they had traveled with him back home to Mauldin that summer, they would have seen otherwise. Kevin spent much of his time at the town recreation center, working with boys from his old high school.

When Kevin returned to Minnesota, he picked up where he had left off. In 1997-98, he averaged 18.5 points, 9.6 rebounds, and 4.2 assists per game. Again, he was selected to the All-Star team. And he helped lead the Wolves back to the playoffs.

But changes were around the corner. When the season

ended, Tom left the team as a free agent to play for the Phoenix Suns. The Wolves decided to rebuild. Midway through the 1998-99 season, they traded Stephon to the New Jersey Nets. The team, stripped of two of its three stars, seemed doomed. That's when Kevin really showed his skill. He had his best season ever, averaging 20.8 points, 10.4 rebounds, and 4.3 assists per game. Almost single-handedly, he led the Wolves back to the playoffs.

Kevin McHale, a former NBA All-Star, was amazed. "When the ball is in his hands, he just lights up," he said. "It's playtime. It's like putting crayons in a kid's hands."

The Wolves lost in the first playoff round to the San Antonio Spurs, who would go on to win the NBA title. But Kevin had established himself as a true force in the league — on the court and off.

The basketball revolutionary had become a superstar.

Kevin's Hall of Fame Double

The only man who came close to Kevin in size and speed was Connie Hawkins. Connie was a star center and forward in the American Basketball Association (ABA) in the 1960's. (The ABA, a rival of the NBA, existed from 1967 to 1976.) Connie joined the NBA in the 1970's and was a four-time All-Star. Like Kevin, Connie ran the court like a guard and was known for his monster dunks. But Kevin is a better ball handler and has a better outside shot.

WANT TO HAVE MORE FUN!

WITH SPORTS ILLUSTRATED FOR KIDS?

GET A FREE TRIAL ISSUE of SPORTS ILLUSTRATED FOR KIDS magazine. Each monthly issue is jam-packed with awesome athletes, super-sized photos, cool sports facts, comics, games, and jokes!

Ask your mom or dad to call and order your free trial issue today! The phone number is 1-800-732-5080.

PLUG IN TO www.sikids.com. That's the S.I. FOR KIDS website on the Internet. You'll find great games, free fantasy leagues, sports news, trivia quizzes, and more. (Tell your mom or dad to check out www.sportsparents.com, too.)

CHECK OUT S.I. FOR KIDS Weekly in the comic section of many newspapers. It has lots of cool photos, stories, and puzzles from the Number 1 sports magazine for kids!

LOOK FOR more S.I. FOR KIDS books. They make reading **fun!**